MAN KILLS GIRLFRIEND OVER COLD SANDWICHES

AND OTHER SAD TALES

poems by

michelle a. johnson

Finishing Line Press
Georgetown, Kentucky

MAN KILLS GIRLFRIEND OVER COLD SANDWICHES

AND OTHER SAD TALES

for weng, cath, chelsea, gabriel & aurora ~
seven generations back and forward.

ACKNOWLEDGMENTS

"After Hours;" "Divorce;" "Cinderella Redux" published in *Suisun Valley Review*
"Sunday Mornings;" "Dead Waitress Order;" "Man Kills Girlfriend over Cold Sandwiches and other Sad Tales;" "Piano Man" published in *Sierra Journal*
"Nebraska Winter, 1983" published in *Calaveras Station*
"Replacement" and "Christmas, 1982" published in *Yuba Review*
"Many are Making Love" published in the *Bazanella Awards*

Publisher: Leah Huete de Maines
Editor: Christen Kincaid
Cover Art and Design: Wendah P. Alvarez
Author Photo: Wendah P. Alvarez

Order online: www.finishinglinepress.com
also available on amazon.com

Author inquiries and mail orders:
Finishing Line Press
P. O. Box 1626
Georgetown, Kentucky 40324
U. S. A.

Table of Contents

INVENTORY
—after reading Dorianne Laux's "What I Wouldn't Do"

First it was Dairy Twist.
All the softserve
I could consume.
Greasy smells of fries and onion curls
soaked through my pores.
Lovestruck teens swapped spit & bubble gum
while waiting for their afterschool shakes.
After that it was Kids Country Careland,
cleaning after a 100 preschoolers.
"Free-art" debris sprinkled wall-to-wall.
The afternoon snacks—regurgitated—in the carpet.
Bartending was fine, blending lime Margaritas,
pouring sugary Manhattans, chilled Cosmopolitans,
& another shot for the bartender.
I drank and packed
my nose from job to job:
The Hacienda where I wore
a sombrero and swallowed
too many Tequilas,
too many men.
Gernot's Schnitzel Haus,
with the oom-pa-pa bands, dark warm beer
& married insurance salesmen.
Omaha Johnny's Steak House,
where I served
corn-fed beef and rooster fries
on a wet leaf of bleached lettuce.
I liked 1-800 Holiday Inn
reservations best.
Grave shift, alone in a corner cubicle,
surrounded by the quiet hum
of resting computer terminals,
radio tuned to KGOR
and my journal opened, ready
to record another life,
not my own.

PLAYING HOUSE

This is about waiting in an unclean room
on scuffdirt gray, and humbling yourself
to ask for temporary help.
This is about feeling guilty
for asking because
you know
if you were a decent American,
you'd get a job—three or four—
if you had to.
You'd forget about going to college.
Forget your child is more familiar
with the back of your head,
always leaving
to another low-paying job.

You sway to and fro, uncomfortably,
shifting your daughter
from one hip to the other.
Your neck tingles
with heated embarrassment.
You wonder how much longer this will take.
You worry what the social workers will think of you:
Just another one milking the system.
Just another lazy oaf, sponging off the tax dollars
of the real, hard working Americans.
You've heard it all before.
You used to think that way, too,
once. Your head
starts to fuzz.
You think you may vomit.

The whines of crying children
and thick phlegmy coughs fill your ears.
You want to
turn away. Do it all.
Go to school, work five jobs,
make heart-shaped strawberry cupcakes
for your daughter's Valentine's party.
But you just can't anymore.
You rub your pounding temples,
closing your eyes to the deafening squall

until you recognize the called name
of an old school playmate
from the fourth grade.
The big brown beauty mark
on her left cheek. Platinum blonde
hair with a little wave.
It's definitely her.
An old friend.

Darla, remember me? Remember when
we used to play house?

She looks through you.
You feel sick again,
as she tugs on the arm
of a whining, snot-nosed kid who wants to go home—NOW.
She stops and yells, "Stop that right now, damn it!"

You decide it's best not to remember.
You just wait
for your name.

JUST A PENNY AWAY

A man cashed in
ten thousand dollars
worth of pennies.
Talk about saving
pennies for a rainy day.

Seems he had a bit
of trouble getting any bank
to take the three ton savings.
Who knew someone could save
for too many rainy days?

                    * * *

If his outdated *Sierra Traders* and *Bowhunter* catalogs,
piles of *Wheels & Deals,*
Penthouse and *Hustler,*
12 ratchet sets, 57 screwdrivers, 5 hammers,
salvaged BeigeBrown paint,
dented cans of Pledge and ACE grime remover,
books showcasing the good life
(but not how to live it),
extendo-magnets, MENSA cards, role-playing die,
3 Peruvian hand-stitched, full-sized indoor hammocks
with holes only one Peruvian can mend
(and she's out of the country for an undetermined amount of time)

If all these things
and so much more
were like three tons of pennies,
imagine the rainbow
in my storm.

IT'S ALWAYS BEEN ABOUT NUMBERS

The ache of them
constantly pressing
in my mind:

Digital green, cyclical ticks and failing red.
Ages, dates, sizes, percentages, weights, measures, times.

Fixed determinations order the outcome of my day.
They can be positive and real—marvelous remainders of fragmented
memories:

34/24/36. . .11/9/88. . .4.0. . .9. . .135.
Even so, they usually signal bad times.

Sequences of threes pop up. They haunt and tease.
These numbers, painful as unrelieved high pitched tones.

I am reminded of the incalculable timing of my grandfather's death.
Weeks prior, an unrelenting sequence of threes presented themselves:
Waking at 3:33am. . .grocery bill $33.33. . .the odometer 33,777.
Several days in March, a new combination of three.
Then he was dead.

Freakish coincidence? Possibly.
Except, Nana saw them too.

Numbers keep me out.
Missed it by one.

Numbers rule the blinding migraines that knock the color out of my face:
Four days before, four days in, or four days after seven days of cramping and
clotting.

Numbers: the total of my debts. The size and weight I wear.
The deciders of my children's intelligence.

Numbers: a reminder of a failing greater than the distance between two
unknowns,
but equal to the lowest common denominator and the highest numerator
leaving me
mixed and improper.

AFTER HOURS

If this sticky bartop
could talk, it would share stories
of nights spent here,
breasting up to the counter,
ordering sexy drinks all night.
It would snitch,
how after hours
you let some name forgotten drunk
lift you up on that bar,
gathering ashes and granules of margarita
   salt.
How you let him drizzle
Rumplemintz, spreading you open
licking you clean.

Your story would be out.
You would witness your husband
hear the news
of how you said you were tending
late, but you weren't.
You were on the other side, here—
licking the inside of your thumb and index
   finger,
shaking the salt,
sucking the lime
to sour the burn of tequila,
carrying you away from the lie.
It would snitch how you leaned
into the man next to you,
young and strange,
who you knew you would fuck
because your marriage was old,
lonely. Another shot would move your
   hands
into his, and before you knew it
the bar would close.

You'd catch a glimpse of your face
in the strips of mirror
between dusted liquor bottles.
You would see yourself as other

because mothers do not service strangers
on countertops after hours.

If this countertop could confess,
it would report
the white lines
you chopped and snorted,
on the sly, off of tip trays
between drinks and handjobs in the back.
Because what the bar does not see, it hears.

If this bar could talk,
it would recount
how pathetic you looked
that night, pleading with him
to take you home. Promising him
it would be the last time.
You would not show up
on his doorstep, drunk
anymore, not come
into his bed and fumble
with his sleeping cock.
You would not
if he would,
just one more time,   *please.*
But he left you there,
swaying unevenly,
emptying another glass.

Luckily for you,
your stories are safe,
wiped clean for the morning shift.

SUNDAY MORNINGS

i leave fresh-squeezed orange juice
and the man where the music is not

and slip out
to where it is everywhere.

jays and dew drops drown out
the weighty silence his voice carries.

i stoop to lift the *Sacramento Bee*
wet from last night's unexpected storm.

i deliver the funnies,
two sunny-side eggs and an overdone biscuit.

it's what he likes first;
then he reads the news:

abandoned baby doe, in the dumpster, dead
in the last bathroom stall—so many babies.

but, he's not much interested in babies
or my aching ovaries, empty uterus and aging nipples.

although, another egg and the Forum
would be just fine, indeed.

i crack the large brown shell,
spill and trace the tiny umbilical thread to heavy yolk

i form a baby in black Teflon
and serve it up on a pale blue platter.

SHARPER IMAGE, INTERRUPTED

I disrupt his intense browsing
with a necklace & a loose robe

draped off my shoulders
the back of my neck revealed—fine hairs & curls invite.

Annoyed, he rises,
carefully marking his slick page,

& fumbles the troubled clasp.
I entertain how hard it would be

to resist this nape.
His breath would grow suddenly hotter closer.

Impatient he would toss the difficult chain
aside & press warm, wet kisses

there & here
I close my eyes

 as a tiny moan just leaves my lips,
"There."

He plops back down,
returns to his catalog.

The strand is tighter.

TOMORROW NEVER COMES
—inspired by Sherwood Anderson's "A Death in the Woods"

There is a story
about an old woman
who isn't really old,
just old because of circumstances
not her own.
(It seems, she is a victim.)
But as stories go,
for women made old
before their time,
she has no concern
for herself and her loneliness.
She has things
to feed,
she has matters
to tend,
she has lives
to nourish—
husband, children, cats and chores
(there is time for bubble baths later.)
And so it goes:
she tends, nourishes and feeds
well into the late of night.
Each child, cat and man
tugs and whines.
Should she turn this way or that?
Always another thing
to feed,
always another matter
to tend,
always another life
demanding & sucking
at her very marrow.
And who else will care
for these things
if she does not?
She has no time
to ponder the alternate possibilities,
for surely,
most certainly,
tomorrow
she will be done.

DIVORCE

I stand on the corner
of Main and B

until the butterscotch moon
bronzes his path of leaving.

Inhaling. Exhaling.
Feeling delicious.

Then almost sinfully erotic,
like stolen heat

from a lust-craved
lover's thighs   pressing hard.

Or the twist-tease-tingle
of a disembodied tongue

journeying the wide open highway
of my spine. Smooth. Intoxicating.

And so,
frozen I stand

locked in sensual moment
breathing effortlessly in tandem

with October breezes and shuffle of drying leaves.
Tugging on the golden band,

I turn hot
in the cold.

MANY ARE MAKING LOVE

but i do not see sensual shadows move
upndown. i do not secretly linger
behind bush and shade to witness

lovers perform their breathy art.
i do not see. but, god, how i can hear
below the buzz of quiet cloudy

night. my, how i can decipher
between electronic hummm and pleasurable "mmmm"
trickling its way out of

a lover's ravenous mouth.
some can see movement in absolute dark
of dense woods. some can already

taste vinegar below the sweet of port &
some can feel out a love impostor from across a crowded
dance floor. i can hear many

making love. having sex. doing it.
at any time of day or night.
it's sort of a quirky gift. a stupid human trick.

i can hear my roommate,
quietly enjoying the latenight flesh
of some nameless barfly

in the bedroom above, and it can
be voyeuristic music when i hear
every sigh. pillowed moan.

i can detect, in a house, supposedly dead asleep,
the sounds of silent screwing.
it wakes me up. preempts sleep.

the creak of spring is not the shift
of sleepers. it is the lift of love moving
into controlled slippery rhythm.

the hush of "mmm" is not the uttering
of dreamers dining on something
delicious. It is the slip of tongue

and parting lip in unrestrained pleasure.
Many are having sex.
I can hear the tear of lubricated foils

the silent sound of synthetic spermicidal
slide—SNAP—into place. I can hear
the wet of her tongue. The rush of his pulse.

In the dark. Alone. I can make out
a violent push. The rip of fragile flesh.
I can hear frightened "nnnns"

that get confused for "mmms"
which precede the "o's."
i can hear his thoughts muffled behind

the slap & slam of headboard against yellowed wallpaper:
I'm pleasin' her. She's into it.
He thinks it is "mmm" (yes)

he know it's "o" (yeah)
(not "NO"; she means "YES")
i am awake and listening, fascinated,

      yet,
sickened by my gift, my hearing.
It keeps me up late at night.

i hear some making love. i hear many
only making out, but never can i seem
to turn down the dissonance.

The loud taking.
Always hearing.
Many are making love.

REPLACEMENT

Love lacking
Cupboards brimming

Today   creamy-thighs wrap'round
orgy of empty Domino's Pizza boxes, while yesterdays'
Hershey's kisses fill them.
M&M replace S&M.

      i don't know how to stop

Compulsion for the consumption-seduction
feverishly feeding
      (chocolate chip cookie fantasy fudge rocky road gallons)
no longer satisfied.

      i'm out of control

always hungry
aching to fill my mouth—
Void of you.

sumptuous piece
of hard candy
      i suck   sweet
creamed confection dripping
taste of you
can't have you, so
i eat—
love—
leftovers.

DATING SERVICES: 20 ME: 0

Steve said he was six feet—
I'm five-eleven—
He barely came to my chin.
Kevin said, *I'm tall and tan.*
A tall black man sat down.
Then there was Ted, who, on *our first date,*
bragged that while providing oral lovin'
he caused his date's foot to crash
through his glass coffee table,
And it was thick glass, too.

Hans was very open to sex
because he molested his little sister—
He was sixteen; she was twelve.
It was only a couple of times.
He was getting help, of course.

Matt said after a decaffeinated espresso,
You're a little too high strung. Busy.
Have you considered Bikram and Soy?
It's very centering.

Over margaritas another confessed
He was still sorta married, but not really.
It was complicated.
Another wasn't married—
he just wanted a good time.
Like how about now?

Wendell said he thought
about getting a dog instead
of a girlfriend. *Dogs are easier.*
David liked to kiss
hard and deep-throat like
and suggest weight-loss tips.

Another enthusiastically proposed
reading up on giving
blowjobs. Good advice
he thought, since many in his past
missed important parts. Tom thought

it was appropriate to tell me
I was very entertaining,
just not very pretty.
B. Love studied reproduction
in honeybees, but felt too much pressure
to balance bees and me.

There was a surgeon, a butcher, a contractor, a metal band bassist,
    a computer engineer and an embezzler.

The embezzler kept a notebook
with sketches of Lionel train setups
he'd like to have some day.
He let me look at the book
while he went to the bathroom.

There was Karl from Ireland.
Partied with Bono. We ate jicama on his backporch,
drank hot tea, and sipped syrah
late into the evening.
We kissed and promised another day.
An email waiting said—
Dating and relationships
take too much work,
don't they? Take care.

The last one fathered six children—
with six different women—
He was only married once.
He flashed two gold teeth,
as he stiffed our server.

My new-aged friends say
happiness and love
are already within us.
I just need to be open.
Send out the positives and love
will find me. And my mom,
she tells me,
Go to church.

MAN KILLS GIRLFRIEND OVER COLD SANDWICHES AND OTHER SAD TALES

Seems perfectly reasonable,
somehow, say when it's been raining
and raining for days and days.
Or when the shitty brown snow
just won't melt, and there's more
in the forecast.
And it's April.

So, I can see how a guy
might get a bit testy
after being shut in, and feel
the need to, say,
chuck a microwave oven
into the chest of his lady friend.
And after she's down,
stomp on her a bit.
Then, after that,
slam her head hard
into the dirty linoleum a few times.

Too, I kind of get how a mom
might get irritated
after darkdays of winter
seepdeep and feel the need
to,   maybe
toss her colicky babe
away. Stick it somewhere,
like in a microwave and wait
for the promise
of a silent thaw
and a tinny "ding."

And there are other times,
when there's no sun in sight,
I can taste electricbile,
as I consider sliding
the broken point
of my kitchen knife
deep into my man's heart—

I don't actually do it,
but some days,
it just seems
perfectly natural.

READING

She stands,
dressed in dramatic black
before a quiet few—
her foot a nervous wobble.

She will read aloud
her poetry to an audience of women.
The first-time poem
of the backdoor nights
her father. . .
and the one about that
preppy star center
and the way
he took. . .
Perhaps she will read
the one where she hisses
shut-up
at her child
she does not always love.
She is unsure.

But she is here
before a few *nice* women
who relate the times
their fathers got too. . .
And of course,
they know the "different" players,
and the under-the-skin-pin-pricking-guilt
when *they* can't love
their own children.

They nod in silent "yeses."
Yes.
These knowing women
and the dry-mouthed poet
will share Chablis-soaked sorrows
and uneasy glances
after words.

Alone, each will depart—
drunk with thick syllables, or a lumpy line

stuck somewhere
between breastbone and throat—
choking.

STALLED

Summer is heavy
with thick scents
of peaches and over-ripe pears.
I want to drive
through the orchards
to avoid the crush
pressing my tiny town.

It's hot,
too hot for a car with no air
I want to drive faster—
like those zippy tv commercial cars
on wide, empty roads—
past the single passenger SUVs
and sputtering Hondas
"riced out" to race.

Away.
But I am stuck,
idling uneasily, as sweat forms
beneath my breasts. There has to be
a crash somewhere.

I consider turning around,
but I have promised the kids
a drive. An overdue afternoon
outing to remember
because my mother-guilt
clings like distant static.

So, I wait,
wondering if I'll have
enough gas to get us there.

CHRISTMAS, 1982

They are dancing in a tiny Sarasota bar. An old Sinatra tune sparks her energy. The music makes her eyes twinkle with youthful delight. So alive in just a small moment.   I marvel as they float alone on a portable dance floor. She glides effortlessly. Never have I seen them together. Like this. So close, so loving. His strong dark skinned hand gently cradles hers while his other presses the small of her back. They are movie dancing. Her faded green eyes are closed as she hums off-key in his ear. But even more captivating than the motion of their union—her legs.

I sit a few booths away. Transfixed. I cannot recall noticing them like this before; despite seeing them shuffle through household chores, motherly tasks, constantly running. I just did not see. They are not long or particularly muscular, nor are they everyday-ordinary. Yet they are—but so graceful the way they carry her through every movement. Subtly shaped in silk stockings. Perhaps it's the way her size sevens know when to change directions with his that draws my attention for the first *real* time. I am entranced.

In a musical moment, she is no longer the one who makes hot oatmeal with cinnamon sugar on first days of school. Not the one who grits crooked teeth when angry, not the woman who cries because her mother is no longer around to make things right. She is not Reverend McKnight's secretary. She is not the woman who drives for hours on airy Indiana roads to help ease the migraines that plague me. She is not my mother anymore.

Under holiday glow, she is transformed into an elegant woman. Separate from anything I have ever known. Smiling sweetly, turning with him on legs I do not recognize—inconspicuously sturdy—supporting the weight of her worries to walk through another year. Sometimes dancing.

NEBRASKA WINTER, 1983

-after reading about the Danny Joe Ebberle and Chris Walden murders

He was quite the smooth talker the way he talked smooth
Like oh, what's the name of that one guy?
He said *babe* he said *yeah* he said *babe* he said *yeah*
Just as they slow-swayed on the sticky clubroom dance floor
Like in that one date movie, oh you know the one.

It was a frozen Omaha night,
snotsticking-your-nose-shut kind of cold.
The kind of cold that freezes foggy screams midair.
The kind Chris might have cried
before Joubert sliced the heavy sound.

He was quite suave the way he asked her to come   y'know
over to his place like that "one" guy.
He said *please* he said *c'mon* he said *please* he said *c'mon*
just after he kissed her Bonne Bell lips in the Midwest chill
like that one scene on that crime show, oh what was it called, that one show,
you know.

It was early morning, or was it late?
Early? Late? It's hard to say when your baby is missing.
The *Omaha World Herald* left in a satchel on the side of the road, waiting to be
            delivered;
just like the cries Danny Joe struggled
to make before Joubert stabbed and stabbed and

He was quite sorry he'd lost his way.
Most sorry they were out of gas in the dark,
like that one prom couple in that one story   you know
He said *c'mere* he said *now* he said *c'mere* he said *now*
As he jammed his sweaty palms between her legs.

It is late September or perhaps early December
Late? Early? It's difficult to say when your baby is missing.
Missing, as in believed to be kidnapped, perhaps raped.
Murdered.   Dead.
Like those two boys,
and that one young girl
who was last seen leaving the NCO Club.
You know the one.

DEAD WAITRESS ORDER
—for those dying to get out of the business

As part of their ascension process, five dead waitresses
come down Purgatory Hill to the abandoned self-serve deli
on the corner of Surf and Beach
to bitch and moan.

An unusual employee meeting
with heavenly results.
Rose calls the final meeting to order.
They begin by listing nameless
wretched, stingy customers
they have haunted:
the "sauces on the sides"
the "well-dones with ketchup"
the "stiffers"
"separate checkers"
and the "we'd-like-it-nows."

They fix dusty deli sandwiches
on left-over, moldy rye.
They suck on dry, wrinkled dills
and pass around dented cans
of warm, flat Falstaff beer.
Betty and Edith rant and rave
while spitting stale Lays and loose teeth.
Seething, they purge memories
of the vacationing rich ones
with polished Gucci shoes,
pink Polos and diamond studded Rolexes:
always so proper, so complimentary, so cheap.

Connie and Judy shudder
at fading memories
of taking pats on the ass
from slick, married stockbrokers
looking for more than just another
cocktail and a bowl of salty nuts.
Rose reminds them:
It wasn't *always* the customer's fault.

On cue, they screech and howl,
exorcising the torturous images

of the unforgiving Bread Nazi at the City Cafe.
Judy struggles to let go of tipstealing
bussers and the paranoid, cocaine-packing baker at Al's Dough and Go.
Rose shakes off the memory of that awful, cranky alcoholic prep cook
sweating stale booze into the frozen vegetable medley at King's Smorga Table.

They pull at remaining netted strands
and nod creaky "yeses."
Connie and Betty touch
throbbing blue and purple
veins on brittle bones.
Edith remembers the fourteen-hour shifts,
swollen ankles and pinched toes.
They all regret
greasy sex on prep tables
with pimply-faced managers.
They cringe with the recollection
of desperate hand jobs on the bar,
in stock rooms among cases of hot Tecate,
and in muggy, small offices thick with Cajun spices,
hopeful for a potential raise and every other Friday off.

Betty remembers the stash vodka in cracked thermoses,
stolen bites of pecan pie and vanilla ice cream
in silent, frozen walk-ins.
They remember the ketchup bottles they should have filled.
The condiments they should have stocked,
guest checks they tore
and the cash they pocketed.
They remember the aprons heavy with change.

And before they clock out
for the very last last time,
they remember that once upon a time,
they had a happy life
outside this diner,
that café,
this spoon & bar.
A life outside *this* deli,
this place,
where five waitresses
came to bitch and moan.

CINDERELLA REDUX

It's time to go,
but I can't find my boots
or my bra.
The room teeters and tips
as I peek under this mess
of sleeping man.

There are traces of him
on my thighs,
on my neck,
in the tangles of my hair,
and I will smell him
as I leave his body
in the twist of his wife's sheets.

I can forget the bra,
but not my Payless suedes.
Not these sassy pull-ons
that dazzled the pants off him
in the Seven Mile House parking lot.

They stayed on until
the room stopped spinning
Then they were tossed off—
                    somewhere.
We settled into a drunken doze,
as Van Morrison skipped the mystic
and a fat cat clawed
at the screen
wanting in.

I need these boots more
than the man because
I have danced for hours
in these sized eight black beauties.
I've crossed countries
and curious states
in this magical footwear.
I've tip-toed and swaggered
in strange cities of robotic-crowds
just to be front row.

These boots design
my emotions—
they make me,
take me
far and away,
more than any prince
ever could.

MS. BULIMIA

I am hungry
for a man.
I want all of him in me—
not just his blue-veined,
pulsing cock.

I start
with the chewy layer
of skin. I peel
it off like the chocolate
icing of a Hostess
cupcake.

My goal: lift without tearing
or ripping—one entire sheet
of man. I twisttwirl transparent tissue
between finger and thumb
and eat it like a sticky fruit rollup.

Next, I cut off bite-sized squares
of plump cheeks,
succulent slices of shank and ass.
First, my bites are measured—
rectangular sections of muscle,
dripping with fat. But,
soon, I become sloppy—ravenous.

It feels like I haven't eaten
in days. I barely pause to chew
the organ sweetmeats.
By the time I swallow
his heart, I know he's mine.

After he's all gone,
there's nothing left
but his neat pile of clothes.
I don't stop there:
Oxford, Dockers, boxers, shoes
find their way to my mouth.
I chew their dryness
to a moist fabric-smack.

It's not about feeling satisfied.
It's sheer consumption. Quantity.
So I turn and search
for more men to gobble.

Shame sets in
when there's no one left.
I'm sick. Full of men.

At first, they don't come
up so easily: bit of ear,
button, strand of flesh.

But with time, and push of rib bone,
I am able to purge them all.
One by one,
they splash
until the bowl is full.

PIANO MAN

When I was a little girl, I had a choice: stay in the car or else
follow him into the NCO club: that crush-red-wall-to-wall-shag-

Pine-Sol-cigarette-smoke-scented hangar. It was a man's
man's bar with a piano and words that stung a young girl's ears.

He'd direct me to a corner Formica table, rounded
with black-pleather and duct-taped chairs. Then he'd give me the look:

This is our secret. Don't tell your mother. Or else. I'd obediently nod and be set
   up
with a Shirley Temple or Roy Rogers, as many as I could drink, and
   sometimes

if I was real quiet and he was in a good mood, I might even get a wooden
   bowl
full of fancy peanuts to eat while he'd *tinkle on the keys* and *shoot the shit.*

Bent forward in concentration, cigarette magically balanced on his lip,
he'd glide his fingers over the yellowed ivory. I was mesmerized.

He'd finish his first drink and holler for another. Then setting it down, he'd
begin taking requests: "Autumn Leaves" "Roll out the Barrel" or *Play that
   one, you know. . .*

Once, when a new bartender wouldn't let me in, I had to wait in the lobby.
   Gulping
my usual sugared beverage, I inhaled a large chunk of ice. Gasping. I knew
I'd die. Alone.

But it melted, so I had to wait for *just one more* smoke, drink, tune. After
   that day,
I often opted to stay in the car until I finished my stack of books,

and gave up believing that he really would *be back in a jiffy.* I'd lift
the silver knobby lock, and peel my sweaty thighs off the seat and creep

toward the patent leather door with buttons and gold script letters. I'd peep
into the smoky air, eyes readjusting to neon light, catching snippets

of my dad's profile swaying back and forth to the music
behind other off-duty soldiers drinking. Once I slipped behind

the juke box, imagining I was Karen Carpenter singing "Rainy Days and
     Mondays"
for the men, and they'd nod, stunned by my sweet, sad song. But now, years
     later,

as I search for the perfect excuse to have *just one more,* I cling to the memory
of the lonely daughter waiting for the piano man's civi-clad body to appear,

with crumpled Marlboro soft-pack in hand, and hearing
his sorry slur say, *Better go get your mom!*

I WONDER (WANDER)

~ Tahoe Forest, La Porte, California, August 2009

Why is it
that woodland critters
don't come out
while I'm strolling
on their piney path?

Surely they must sniff
my desire to stroke
their spotted furs,
look into their doe-eyes
and let them know
I come in peace.

Unlike the Disney girls
before me,
I do not meet
my furry friends
in a clearing as I hum
a little smiley tune.
No cuddly circles form
to enlighten me
of my sweet prince's arrival—
no squeaks of warning
of old women bearing
poisonous fruits or spells
to cast off my sadness.

Instead only the snap
of drying timber marks
my solitary hike.

They must see
from their wooded homes
I do not wield a weapon,
or dream of venison,

skinned, tenderized, smoked
served on bed of pilaf. I do not
skewer twisty worms
on heart impaling hooks

hoping to snatch some
tremendous, ancient fish.

I simply long
to commune with them.
Unearth sweet, dew dotted
berries in woody nooks.
Share warm morning sun
on a smooth rock
near Pancake Bay.
Meet drowsy buzzards
on Eagle Tree.
It'd be such fun
to return the squeaks
and scratchy chirps of ground squirrels,
confirming my presence.

I'd like to honk and quack
with the Canadians and Mallards,
and ask how they manage
to stay with one mate
                    for life,
especially since I
can't last more than seven years.

I want them
to come to my rented cabin
to be safe from man-
made wildfires burning
in their Yuba hills.

DO WORMS SURFACE

in spring storms
to avoid their flooding
underground passages?
And after the rain
do they linger too long—too late

caught by the afterheat,
their multi-hearted bodies
toughen to jerky bits
of their former succulent selves?

Even though they no longer
writhe with life, we are careful
not to step on them.

Perhaps there is just one
heart left—still beating.

Imagine a little girl
who stays up late,
worrying for the worms.
She designs a plan
to save them all.

Donned in a squeaky yellow
slicker, she braves
morning drops
and carefully collects
the squirming squidlettes.
She places them in a hollow notch
tree home, padded with cushy
green moss and a matchbox TV.

For hours, she checks in
her five-hearted friends
until it is booked to capacity.
Her mother calls
her inside. From the kitchen,
she waits for the rain to end.

I BELIEVE

words evade and often save,
like a touch.
I believe in me &
the power of guilt.
I believe I am a good person
even though I lie daily.
I know I am a bitch
of a wife;
I expect too much.
I am never satisfied.
I believe food is evil,
and cocktails are not much better.
I believe Mom and Dad believe
they are excellent parents.
I believe I will never share their beliefs.
I believe my daughter would be disappointed
if she knew who I really was;
my son already knows.
I believe cats have easy lives;
cows and chickens do not.
Mostly, I believe
Hell is here on Earth,
and Heaven is when we finally get
to float away to some place else where Hell isn't.
I believe there are too many stores
packed with too many things
we do not need,
especially when people away
sway in line for days to have a chance
at two bruised apples and a roll of scratchy toilet paper.
I believe it's easy to believe
things will never run out—
not here
in America.

I fantasize old lovers remember my name,
and some even call it out by mistake
when they're with their significant others.
Believe me, that makes me smile.
Everything I think
I know is right today,

will be wrong tomorrow.
Someday
I want to understand
how love works and
get it right.
I have to believe
I am not finished.

CPSIA information can be obtained
at www.ICGtesting.com
Printed in the USA
LVHW090239181120
672018LV00005B/158

9 781646 623419